HOLES IN THE SKY

Books
By Louis MacNeice

*

POEMS

THE EARTH COMPELS

PLANT AND PHANTOM

AUTUMN JOURNAL

SPRINGBOARD

OUT OF THE PICTURE

CHRISTOPHER COLUMBUS

THE DARK TOWER

AGAMEMNON OF AESCHYLUS
(translation)

LETTERS FROM ICELAND
(with W. H. *Auden)*

*

LOUIS MACNEICE

HOLES
IN THE
SKY

Poems 1944-1947

RANDOM HOUSE · NEW YORK

FIRST PRINTING

Some of these poems have previously appeared in *The Bell,*
Horizon, The Irish Times, Lagan, New Writing and Daylight,
Orion, Orpheus, Penguin New Writing, and *Irish Writing.*

What is truth? says Pilate,
Waits for no answer;
Double your stakes, says the clock
To the ageing dancer;
Double the guard, says Authority,
Treble the bars;
Holes in the sky, says the child
Scanning the stars.

CONTENTS

HOLES IN THE SKY

NOTE

'The Streets of Laredo' (pronounced Lareedo) is the name of an American cowboy song. The original tune was specially arranged by William Alwyn so that the poem printed here could be sung by my wife Hedli Anderson.

THE STREETS OF LAREDO

O early one morning I walked out like Agag,
Early one morning to walk through the fire
Dodging the pythons that leaked on the pavements
With tinkle of glasses and tangle of wire;

When grimed to the eyebrows I met an old fireman
Who looked at me wryly and thus did he say:
'The streets of Laredo are closed to all traffic,
We won't never master this joker to-day.

'O hold the branch tightly and wield the axe brightly,
The bank is in powder, the banker's in hell,
But loot is still free on the streets of Laredo
And when we drive home we drive home on the bell.'

Then out from a doorway there sidled a cockney,
A rocking-chair rocking on top of his head:
'O fifty-five years I been feathering my love-nest
And look at it now—why, you'd sooner be dead.'

At which there arose from a wound in the asphalt,
His big wig a-smoulder, Sir Christopher Wren
Saying: 'Let them make hay of the streets of Laredo;
When your ground-rents expire I will build them again.'

Then twangling their bibles with wrath in their nostrils
From Bunhill Fields came Bunyan and Blake:
'Laredo the golden is fallen, is fallen;
Your flame shall not quench nor your thirst shall not slake.'

'I come to Laredo to find me asylum,'
Says Tom Dick and Harry the Wandering Jew;
'They tell me report at the first police station
But the station is pancaked—so what can I do?'

[3]

Thus eavesdropping sadly I strolled through Laredo
Perplexed by the dicta misfortunes inspire
Till one low last whisper inveigled my earhole—
The voice of the Angel, the voice of the fire:

O late, very late, have I come to Laredo
A whimsical bride in my new scarlet dress
But at last I took pity on those who were waiting
To see my regalia and feel my caress.

Now ring the bells gaily and play the hose daily,
Put splints on your legs, put a gag on your breath;
O you streets of Laredo, you streets of Laredo,
Lay down the red carpet—My dowry is death.

HIATUS

The years that did not count—Civilians in the towns
Remained at the same age as in Nineteen-Thirty-Nine,
Saying last year, meaning the last of peace;
Yet eyes began to pucker, mouth to crease,
The hiatus was too packed with fears and frowns,
The would-be absent heart came forth a magnetic mine.

As if the weekly food queue were to stretch,
Absorb all future Europe. Or as if
The sleepers in the Tube had come from Goya's Spain
Or Thucydides' Corcyra—a long way to fetch
People to prove that civilization is vain,
Wrapped in old quilts; no wonder they wake stiff.

Yes, we wake stiff and older; especially when
The schoolboys of the Thirties reappear,
Fledged in the void, indubitably men,
Having kept vigil on the Unholy Mount
And found some dark and tentative things made clear,
Some clear made dark, in the years that did not count.

CORNER SEAT

Suspended in a moving night
The image in the next-door train
Looks at first sight as self-assured
As you do, traveller. Look again:

Windows between you and the world
Keep out the cold, keep out the fright;
Then why does your reflection seem
So lonely in the moving night?

AFTERMATH

Shuffle and cut. What was so large and one
Is now a pack of dog's-eared chances—Oh
Where is the Fear that warmed us to the gun,
That moved the cock to tousle the night and crow
In the gaps between the bombs? In this new round
The joker that could have been any moment death
Has been withdrawn, the cards are what they say
And none is wild; the bandaging dark which bound
This town together is loosed and in the array
Of bourgeois lights man's love can save its breath:
Their ransomed future severs once more the child
Of luck from the child of lack—and none is wild.

TWELFTH NIGHT

Snow-happy hicks of a boy's world—
O crunch of bull's-eyes in the mouth,
O crunch of frost beneath the foot—
If time would only remain furled
In white, and thaw were not for certain
And snow would but stay put, stay put!

When the pillar-box wore a white bonnet—
O harmony of roof and hedge,
O parity of sight and thought—
And each flake had your number on it
And lives were round for not a number
But equalled nought, but equalled nought!

But now the sphinx must change her shape—
O track that reappears through slush,
O broken riddle, burst grenade—
And lives must be pulled out like tape
To measure something not themselves,
Things not given but made, but made.

For now the time of gifts is gone—
O boys that grow, O snows that melt,
O bathos that the years must fill—
Here is dull earth to build upon
Undecorated; we have reached
Twelfth Night or what you will . . . you will.

BLUEBELLS

She, who last felt young during the war,
This Easter has no peace to be waiting for;
Though coining dandelions from her eyes
Has lost the old enrichment of surprise
And though her man is back, yet feels he has brought
The Desert with him, making her cheeks taut.

So both wake early, listen without words
To the now foreign badinage of birds,
And in the twilight when only the bats fly
They miss those engines overbrimming the sky,
For all green Nature has gone out of gear
Since they were apart and hoping, since last year.

Sun is too bright and brittle, wheat is too quick,
She turns from them to the wood where the slow thick
Shade is becalmed and chill and as a glacial stream
Meeting the sea inlays and weaves a milky gleam
Through the dark waste, so here the bluebells flow
Athwart the undergrowth, a merger of blue snow.

'Oh in this dark beneathness where he and I
Live, let a delta of flowers atone for the sky
Which we cannot face and from my ice-cap, oh,
Let one river at least unfreeze and flow
And through that brine so deep and yet so dim
Let my cold gentleness irradiate him.'

TAM CARI CAPITIS

That the world will never be quite—what a cliché—the same
    again
Is what we only learn by the event
When a friend dies out on us and is not there
To share the periphery of a remembered scent

Or leave his thumb-print on a shared ideal;
Yet it is not at floodlit moments we miss him most,
Not intervolution of wind-rinsed plumage of oat-field
Nor curragh dancing off a primeval coast

Nor the full strings of passion; it is in killing
Time where he could have livened it, such as the drop-by-drop
Of games like darts or chess, turning the faucet
On full at a threat to the queen or double top.

THE NATIONAL GALLERY

The kings who slept in the caves are awake and out,
The pictures are back in the Gallery; Old Masters twirl their
    cadenzas, whisper and shout,
Hundreds of windows are open again on a vital but changeless
    world—a day-dream free from doubt.

Here are the angels playing their lutes at the Birth—
Clay become porcelain; the pattern, the light, the ecstasy which
    make sense of the earth;
Here is Gethsemane scooped like a glacier, here is Calvary
    calmly assured of its own worth.

Here are the gold haloes, opaque as coins,
The pink temple of icing-sugar, the blandly scalloped rock which
    joins
Primitive heaven and earth; here is our Past wiping the smuts
    from his eyes, girding his loins.

Here saint may be gorgeous, hedonist austere,
The soul's nativity drawn of the earth and earthy, our brother
    the Ass being near,
The petty compartments of life thrown wind-wide open, our
    lopsided instincts and customs atoned for here.

Here only too have the senses unending joy:
Draperies slip but slip no further and expectation cannot cloy;
The great Venetian buttocks, the great Dutch bosoms, remain
    in their time—their prime—beyond alloy.

And the Painter's little daughter, far-off-eyed,
Still stretches for the cabbage white, her sister dawdling at her
    side;
That she grew up to be mad does not concern us, the idyl and
    the innocent poise abide.

Aye; the kings are back from their caves in the Welsh hills,
Refreshed by darkness, armed with colour, sleight-of-hand and
    imponderables,
Armed with Uccello's lances, with beer-mugs, dragons' tongues,
    peacocks' eyes, bangles and spangles and flounces and frills;

Armed with the full mystique of the commonplace,
The lusts of the eye, the gullet, the loins, the memory—grace
    after living and grace
Before some plain-clothes death grabs at the artist's jemmy,
    leaves us yet one more half-solved case.

For the quickness of the heart deceives the eye,
Reshuffling the themes: a Still Life lives while portrayed flesh
    and feature die
Into fugues and subterfuges of being as enveloping and as aloof
    as a frosty midnight sky.

So fling wide the windows, this window and that, let the air
Blowing from times unconfined to Then, from places further
    and fuller than There,
Purge our particular time-bound unliving lives, rekindle a pente-
    cost in Trafalgar Square.

LITTORAL

Indigo, mottle of purple and amber, ink,
Damson whipped with cream, improbable colours of sea
And unanalysable rhythms—fingering foam
Tracing, erasing its runes, regardless
Of you and me
And whether we think it escape or the straight way home.

The sand here looks like metal, it feels there like fur,
The wind films the sand with sand;
This hoary beach is burgeoning with minutiae
Like a philosopher
Who, thinking, makes cat's-cradles with string—or a widow
Who knits for her sons but remembers a tomb in another land.

Brain-bound or heart-bound sea—old woman or old man—
To whom we are ciphers, creatures to ignore,
We poach from you what images we can,
Luxuriously afraid
To plump the Unknown in a bucket with a spade—
Each child his own seashore.

THE CROMLECH

From trivia of froth and pollen
White tufts in the rabbit warren
And every minute like a ticket
Nicked and dropped, nicked and dropped,
Extracters and abstracters ask
What emerges, what survives,
And once the stopper is unstopped
What was the essence in the flask
And what is Life apart from lives
And where, apart from fact, the value.

To which we answer, being naïve,
Wearing the world upon our sleeve,
That to dissect a given thing
Unravelling its complexity
Outrages its simplicity
For essence is not merely core
And each event implies the world,
A centre needs periphery.

This being so, at times at least
Granted the sympathetic pulse
And granted the perceiving eye
Each pregnant with a history,
Appearance and appearances—
In spite of the philosophers
With their jejune dichotomies—
Can be at times reality.

So Tom and Tessy holding hands
(Dare an abstraction steal a kiss?)
Cannot be generalized away,
Reduced by bleak analysis
To pointers demonstrating laws
Which drain the colour from the day;

Not mere effects of a crude cause
But of themselves significant,
To rule-of-brain recalcitrant,
This that they are and do is This . . .

Tom is here, Tessy is here
At this point in a given year
With all this hour's accessories,
A given glory—and to look
That gift-horse in the mouth will prove
Or disprove nothing of their love
Which is as sure intact a fact,
Though young and supple, as what stands
Obtuse and old, in time congealed,
Behind them as they mingle hands—
Self-contained, unexplained,
The cromlech in the clover field.

CARRICK REVISITED

Back to Carrick, the castle as plumb assured
As thirty years ago—Which war was which?
Here are new villas, here is a sizzling grid
But the green banks are as rich and the lough as hazily lazy
And the child's astonishment not yet cured.

Who was—and am—dumbfounded to find myself
In a topographical frame—here, not there—
The channels of my dreams determined largely
By random chemistry of soil and air;
Memories I had shelved peer at me from the shelf.

Fog-horn, mill-horn, corncrake and church bell
Half-heard through boarded time as a child in bed
Glimpses a brangle of talk from the floor below
But cannot catch the words. Our past we know
But not its meaning—whether it meant well.

Time and place—our bridgeheads into reality
But also its concealment! Out of the sea
We land on the Particular and lose
All other possible bird's-eye views, the Truth
That is of Itself for Itself—but not for me.

Torn before birth from where my fathers dwelt,
Schooled from the age of ten to a foreign voice,
Yet neither western Ireland nor southern England
Cancels this interlude; what chance misspelt
May never now be righted by my choice.

Whatever then my inherited or acquired
Affinities, such remains my childhood's frame
Like a belated rock in the red Antrim clay
That cannot at this era change its pitch or name—
And the pre-natal mountain is far away.

SLUM SONG

O the slums of Dublin fermenting with children
  Wander far and near
The growing years are a cruel squadron
And poverty is a rusty cauldron
  Wander near and far.

The youths play cards by the broken fanlight
  Wander far and near
The Jack looks greasy in the sunlight
As hands will fumble in the moonlight
  Wander near and far.

And the grown man must play the horses
  Wander far and near
Some do better on different courses
But the blacks will remain to draw the hearses
  Wander near and far.

The bowsey in his second childhood
  Wander far and near
Thumbs his pipe of peace and briarwood
But lacks a light to relight his manhood
  Wander near and far.

Near and far, far and near,
The street-lamp winks, the mutes are here,
Above the steeple hangs a star
So near and far . . . far.

THE STRAND

White Tintoretto clouds beneath my naked feet,
This mirror of wet sand imputes a lasting mood
To island truancies; my steps repeat

Someone's who now has left such strands for good
Carrying his boots and paddling like a child,
A square black figure whom the horizon understood—

My father. Who for all his responsibly compiled
Account books of a devout, precise routine
Kept something in him solitary and wild,

So loved the western sea and no tree's green
Fulfilled him like these contours of Slievemore
Menaun and Croaghaun and the bogs between.

Sixty-odd years behind him and twelve before,
Eyeing the flange of steel in the turning belt of brine
It was sixteen years ago he walked this shore

And the mirror caught his shape which catches mine
But then as now the floor-mop of the foam
Blotted the bright reflections—and no sign

Remains of face or feet when visitors have gone home.

LAST BEFORE AMERICA

A spiral of green hay on the end of a rake:
The moment is sweat and sun-prick—children and old women
Big in a tiny field, midgets against the mountain,
So toy-like yet so purposed you could take
This for the Middle Ages.

At night the accordion melts in the wind from the sea
From the bourne of emigrant uncle and son, a defeated
Music that yearns and abdicates; chimney-smoke and spindrift
Mingle and part as ghosts do. The decree
Of the sea's divorce is final.

Pennsylvania or Boston? It was another name,
A land of a better because an impossible promise
Which split these families; it was to be a journey
Away from death—yet the travellers died the same
As those who stayed in Ireland.

Both myth and seismic history have been long suppressed
Which made and unmade Hy Brasil—now an image
For those who despise charts but find their dream's endorsement
In certain long low islets snouting towards the west
Like cubs that have lost their mother.

WESTERN LANDSCAPE

In doggerel and stout let me honour this country
Though the air is so soft that it smudges the words
And herds of great clouds find the gaps in the fences
Of chance preconceptions and foam-quoits on rock-points
At once hit and miss, hit and miss.
So the kiss of the past is narcotic, the ocean
Lollingly lullingly over-insidiously
Over and under crossing the eyes
And docking the queues of the teetotum consciousness
Proves and disproves what it wants.
For the western climate is Lethe,
The smoky taste of cooking on turf is lotus,
There are affirmation and abnegation together
From the broken bog with its veins of amber water,
From the distant headland, a sphinx's fist, that barely grips the
    sea,
From the taut-necked donkey's neurotic-asthmatic-erotic lament-
    ing,
From the heron in trance and in half-mourning,
From the mitred mountain weeping shale.

O grail of emerald passing light
And hanging smell of sweetest hay
And grain of sea and loom of wind
Weavingly laughingly leavingly weepingly—
Webs that will last and will not.
But what
Is the hold upon, the affinity with
Ourselves of such a light and line,
How do we find continuance
Of our too human skeins of wish
In this inhuman effluence?
O relevance of cloud and rock—
If such could be our permanence!
The flock of mountain sheep belong

To tumbled screes, to tumbling seas
The ribboned wrack, and moor to mist;
But we who savour longingly
This plenitude of solitude
Have lost the right to residence,
Can only glean ephemeral
Ears of our once beatitude.
Caressingly cajolingly—
Take what you can for soon you go—
Consolingly, coquettishly,
The soft rain kisses and forgets,
Silken mesh on skin and mind;
A deaf-dumb siren that can sing
With fingertips her falsities,
Welcoming, abandoning.

O Brandan, spindrift hermit, who
Hankering roaming un-homing up-anchoring
From this rock wall looked seawards to
Knot the horizon round your waist,
Distil that distance and undo
Time in a quintessential West:
The best negation, round as nought,
Stiller than stolen sleep—though bought
With mortification, voiceless choir
Where all were silent as one man
And all desire fulfilled, unsought.
Thought:
The curragh went over the wave and dipped in the trough
When that horny-handed saint with the abstract eye set off
Which was fourteen hundred years ago—maybe never—
And yet he bobs beyond that next high crest for ever.
Feeling:
Sea met sky, he had neither floor nor ceiling,
The rising blue of turf-smoke and mountain were left behind,
Blue neither upped nor downed, there was blue all round the
    mind.

Emotion:
One thought of God, one feeling of the ocean,
Fused in the moving body, the unmoved soul,
Made him a part of a not to be parted whole.
Whole.
And the West was all the world, the lonely was the only,
The chosen—and there was no choice—the Best,
For the beyond was here . . .

                                        But for us now
The beyond is still out there as on tiptoes here we stand
On promontories that are themselves a-tiptoe
Reluctant to be land. Which is why this land
Is always more than matter—as a ballet
Dancer is more than body. The west of Ireland
Is brute and ghost at once. Therefore in passing
Among these shadows of this permanent show
Flitting evolving dissolving but never quitting—
This arbitrary and necessary Nature
Both bountiful and callous, harsh and wheedling—
Let now the visitor, although disfranchized
In the constituencies of quartz and bog-oak
And ousted from the elemental congress,
Let me at least in token that my mother
Earth was a rocky earth with breasts uncovered
To suckle solitary intellects
And limber instincts, let me, if a bastard
Out of the West by urban civilization
(Which unwished father claims me—so I must take
What I can before I go) let me who am neither Brandan
Free of all roots nor yet a rooted peasant
Here add one stone to the indifferent cairn . . .
With a stone on the cairn, with a word on the wind, with a
    prayer in the flesh let me honour this country.

UNDER THE MOUNTAIN

Seen from above
The foam in the curving bay is a goose-quill
That feathers . . . unfeathers . . . itself.

Seen from above
The field is a flap and the haycocks buttons
To keep it flush with the earth.

Seen from above
The house is a silent gadget whose purpose
Was long since obsolete.

But when you get down
The breakers are cold scum and the wrack
Sizzles with stinking life.

When you get down
The field is a failed or a worth-while crop, the source
Of back-ache if not heartache.

And when you get down
The house is a maelstrom of loves and hates where you—
Having got down—belong.

NO MORE SEA

Dove-melting mountains, ridges gashed with water,
Itinerant clouds whose rubrics never alter,
Give, without oath, their testimony of silence
To islanders whose hearts themselves are islands;

For whom, if the ocean bed should silt up later
And living thoughts coagulate in matter,
An age of mainlanders, that dare not fancy
Life out of uniform, will feel no envy—

No envy unless some atavistic scholar
Plodding that dry and tight-packed world discover
Some dusty relic that once could swim, a fossil
Mind in its day both its own king and castle,

And thence conceive a vague inaccurate notion
Of what it meant to live embroiled with ocean
And between moving dunes and beyond reproving
Sentry-boxes to have been self-moving.

GODFATHER

Elusive
This godfather who mostly forgets one's birthday,
Perusing
Old schoolbooks when he should be reading the papers
Or, when he does
Glance at a daily, snooping between the headlines.

Revolving
Doors whisk him away as you enter a café,
Clopping
Hoofs of black horses drown his steps in the High Street;
He signs
Huge cheques without thinking, never is overdrawn.

The air-raids
Found him lying alone on his back and blowing
Carefree
Smoke-rings—a pipe-dream over the burning city;
At the crack
Of dawn he would lounge away, his hands in his pockets.

Adept
At all surprises, disguises, to conjure a Christmas
Packet
Into a stocking unnoticed or make without fussing
His first call ever and leave
Pale stone tablets like visiting cards in the churchyard.

AUBADE FOR INFANTS

Snap the blind; I am not blind,
I must spy what stalks behind
Wall and window—Something large
Is barging up beyond the down,
Chirruping, hooting, hot of foot.

Beyond that wall what things befall?
My eye can fly though I must crawl.
Dance and dazzle—Something bright
Ignites the dumps of sodden cloud,
Loud and laughing, a fiery face . . .

Whose broad grimace (the voice is bass)
Makes nonsense of my time and place—
Maybe you think that I am young?
I who flung before my birth
To mother earth the dawn-song too!

And you—
However old and deaf this year—
Were near me when that song was sung.

THE CYCLIST

Freewheeling down the escarpment past the unpassing horse
Blazoned in chalk the wind he causes in passing
Cools the sweat of his neck, making him one with the sky,
In the heat of the handlebars he grasps the summer
Being a boy and to-day a parenthesis
Between the horizon's brackets; the main sentence
Is to be picked up later but these five minutes
Are all to-day and summer. The dragonfly
Rises without take-off, horizontal,
Underlining itself in a sliver of peacock light.

And glaring, glaring white
The horse on the down moves within his brackets,
The grass boils with grasshoppers, a pebble
Scutters from under the wheel and all this country
Is spattered white with boys riding their heat-wave,
Feet on a narrow plank and hair thrown back
And a surf of dust beneath them. Summer, summer—
They chase it with butterfly nets or strike it into the deep
In a little red ball or gulp it lathered with cream
Or drink it through closed eyelids; until the bell
Left-right-left gives his forgotten sentence
And reaching the valley the boy must pedal again
Left-right-left but meanwhile
For ten seconds more can move as the horse in the chalk
Moves unbeginningly calmly
Calmly regardless of tenses and final clauses
Calmly unendingly moves.

WOODS

My father who found the English landscape tame
Had hardly in his life walked in a wood,
Too old when first he met one; Malory's knights,
Keats's nymphs or the Midsummer Night's Dream
Could never arras the room, where he spelled out True and Good,
With their interleaving of half-truths and not-quites.

While for me from the age of ten the socketed wooden gate
Into a Dorset planting, into a dark
But gentle ambush, was an alluring eye;
Within was a kingdom free from time and sky,
Caterpillar webs on the forehead, danger under the feet,
And the mind adrift in a floating and rustling ark

Packed with birds and ghosts, two of every race,
Trills of love from the picture-book—Oh might I never land
But here, grown six foot tall, find me also a love
Also out of the picture-book; whose hand
Would be soft as the webs of the wood and on her face
The wood-pigeon's voice would shaft a chrism from above.

So in a grassy ride a rain-filled hoof-mark coined
By a finger of sun from the mint of Long Ago
Was the last of Lancelot's glitter. Make-believe dies hard;
That the rider passed here lately and is a man we know
Is still untrue, the gate to Legend remains unbarred,
The grown-up hates to divorce what the child joined.

Thus from a city when my father would frame
Escape, he thought, as I do, of bog or rock
But I have also this other, this English, choice
Into what yet is foreign; whatever its name
Each wood is the mystery and the recurring shock
Of its dark coolness is a foreign voice.

Yet in using the word tame my father was maybe right,
These woods are not the Forest; each is moored
To a village somewhere near. If not of to-day
They are not like the wilds of Mayo, they are assured
Of their place by men; reprieved from the neolithic night
By gamekeepers or by Herrick's girls at play.

And always we walk out again. The patch
Of sky at the end of the path grows and discloses
An ordered open air long ruled by dyke and fence,
With geese whose form and gait proclaim their consequence,
Pargetted outposts, windows browed with thatch,
And cow pats—and inconsequent wild roses.

WEEK-END

Clink—as a moth collides with a bulb of light;
The tiny sound like an unexpected comma
Breaks the first paragraph of their country night,
Sending them back to the start of the leisurely sentence—
Now where were they? Did they not frame it right?

This week-end, billed as a self-contained romance
Entirely their own composition—but they never
Saw any proofs—is suddenly seen askance
And found askew; the owls beyond the window
Know too much, the trees have changed their stance

As if they meant to grapple. Can it be true
That even so new, so nameless, a pair of lovers
Wishing to blend their persons in Me-and-You
Has excited the envy, the retribution of Nature?
This is a difficult period to construe.

'We were joint authors and the page was white,
We wanted the print to flow like a virgin river
Undammed by punctuation but in despite
Of our inner world the outer made its ingress
When Something rang an alarm upon the light.'

ELEGY FOR MINOR POETS

Who often found their way to pleasant meadows
Or maybe once to a peak, who saw the Promised Land,
Who took the correct three strides but tripped their hurdles,
Who had some prompter they barely could understand,
Who were too happy or sad, too soon or late,
I would praise these in company with the Great;

For if not in the same way, they fingered the same language
According to their lights. For them as for us
Chance was a coryphaeus who could be either
An angel or an *ignis fatuus*.
Let us keep our mind open, our fingers crossed;
Some who go dancing through dark bogs are lost.

Who were lost in many ways, through comfort, lack of knowl-
    edge,
Or between women's breasts, who thought too little, too much,
Who were the world's best talkers, in tone and rhythm
Superb, yet as writers lacked a sense of touch,
So either gave up or just went on and on—
Let us salute them now their chance is gone;

And give the benefit of the doubtful summer
To those who worshipped the sky but stayed indoors
Bound to a desk by conscience or by the spirit's
Hayfever. From those office and study floors
Let the sun clamber on to the notebook, shine,
And fill in what they groped for between each line.

Who were too carefree or careful, who were too many
Though always few and alone, who went the pace
But ran in circles, who were lamed by fashion,
Who lived in the wrong time or the wrong place,
Who might have caught fire had only a spark occurred,
Who knew all the words but failed to achieve the Word—

Their ghosts are gagged, their books are library flotsam,
Some of their names—not all—we learnt in school
But, life being short, we rarely read their poems,
Mere source-books now to point or except a rule,
While those opinions which rank them high are based
On a wish to be different or on lack of taste.

In spite of and because of which, we later
Suitors to their mistress (who, unlike them, stays young)
Do right to hang on the grave of each a trophy
Such as, if solvent, he would himself have hung
Above himself; these debtors preclude our scorn—
Did we not underwrite them when we were born?

AUTOLYCUS

In his last phase when hardly bothering
To be a dramatist, the Master turned away
From his taut plots and complex characters
To tapestried romances, conjuring
With rainbow names and handfuls of sea-spray
And from them turned out happy Ever-afters.

Eclectic always, now extravagant,
Sighting his matter through a timeless prism
He ranged his classical bric-à-brac in grottos
Where knights of Ancient Greece had Latin mottoes
And fishermen their flapjacks—none should want
Colour for lack of an anachronism.

A gay world certainly though pocked and scored
With childish horrors and a fresh world though
Its mainsprings were old gags—babies exposed,
Identities confused and queens to be restored;
But when the cracker bursts it proves as you supposed—
Trinket and moral tumble out just so.

Such innocence—In his own words it was
Like an old tale, only that where time leaps
Between acts three and four there was something born
Which made the stock-type virgin dance like corn
In a wind that having known foul marshes, barren steps,
Felt therefore kindly towards Marinas, Perditas . . .

Thus crystal learned to talk. But Shakespeare balanced it
With what we knew already, gabbing earth
Hot from Eastcheap—Watch your pockets when
That rogue comes round the corner, he can slit
Purse-strings as quickly as his maker's pen
Will try your heartstrings in the name of mirth.

O master pedlar with your confidence tricks,
Brooches, pomanders, broadsheets and what-have-you,
Who hawk such entertainment but rook your client
And leave him brooding, why should we forgive you
Did we not know that, though more self-reliant
Than we, you too were born and grew up in a fix?

STREET SCENE

Between March and April when barrows of daffodils butter the
    pavement,
The colossus of London stretches his gaunt legs, jerking
The smoke of his hair back from his eyes and puffing
Smoke-rings of heavenward pigeons over Saint Paul's,
While in each little city of each individual person
The black tree yearns for green confetti and the black kerb for
    yellow stalls.

Ave Maria! A sluice is suddenly opened
Making Orchard Street a conduit for a fantastic voice;
The Canadian sergeant turns to stone in his swagger,
The painted girls, the lost demobbed, the pinstriped accountant
    listen
As the swan-legged cripple straddled on flightless wings of
    crutches
Hitting her top note holds our own lame hours in equipoise,

Then waddles a yard and switches *Cruising down the river*
Webbed feet hidden, the current smooth *On a Sunday after-*
    noon
Sunshine fortissimo; some young man from the Desert
Fumbles, new from battle-dress, for his pocket,
Drops a coin in that cap she holds like a handbag,
Then slowly walks out of range of *A sentimental tune*

Which cruising down—repeat—cruises down a river
That has no source nor sea but is each man's private dream
Remote as his listening eyes; repeat for all will listen
Cruising away from thought with *An old accordion playing*
Not that it is, her accompanist plucks a banjo
On a Sunday afternoon. She ends. And the other stream

Of Orchard Street flows back—instead of silence racket,
Brakes gears and sparrows; the passers-by pass by,

The swan goes home on foot, a girl takes out her compact—
Silence instead of song; the Canadian dives for the pub
And a naval officer on the traffic island
Unsees the buses with a mid-ocean eye.

RELICS

Obsolete as books in leather bindings
Buildings in stone like talkative ghosts continue
    Their well-worn anecdotes
As here in Oxford shadow the dark-weathered
Astrakhan rustication of the arches
    Puts a small world in quotes:

While high in Oxford sunlight playfully crocketed
Pinnacles, ripe as corn on the cob, look over
    To downs where once without either wheel or hod
Ant-like, their muscles cracking under the sarsen,
Shins white with chalk and eyes dark with necessity
    The Beaker People pulled their weight of God.

THE DRUNKARD

His last train home is Purgatory in reverse,
A spiral back into time and down towards Hell
Clutching a quizzical strap where wraiths of faces
Contract, expand, revolve, impinge; disperse
On a sickly wind which drives all wraiths pell-mell
Through tunnels to their appointed, separate places.

And he is separate too, who had but now ascended
Into the panarchy of created things
Wearing his halo cocked, full of good will
That need not be implemented; time stood still
As the false coin rang and the four walls had wings
And instantly the Natural Man was mended.

Instantly and it would be permanently
God was uttered in words and gulped in gin,
The barmaid was a Madonna, the adoration
Of the coalman's breath was myrrh, the world was We
And pissing under the stars an act of creation
While the low hills lay purring round the inn.

Such was the absolute moment, to be displaced
By moments; the clock takes over—time to descend
Where Time will brief us, briefed himself to oppress
The man who looks and finds Man human and not his friend
And whose tongue feels around and around but cannot taste
That hour-gone sacrament of drunkenness.

HANDS AND EYES

In a high wind
Gnarled hands cup to kindle an old briar,
From a frilled cot
Twin sea anemones grope for a hanging lamp,
In a foul cage
Old coal-gloves dangle from dejected arms.

Of which three pairs of hands the child's are helpless
(Whose wheels barely engage)
And the shepherd's from his age are almost bloodless
While the chimpanzee's are hopeless
Were there not even a cage.

In a dark room
Docile pupils grow to their full for prey,
Down a long bar
Mascara scrawls a gloss on a torn leaf,
On a high col
The climber's blue marries the blue he climbs.

Of which three pairs of eyes the tart's are mindless
(Who pawned her mind elsewhere)
And the black cat's, in gear with black, are heartless
While the alpinist's are timeless
In gear with timeless air.

In a cold church
It flickers in the draught, then burns erect;
In a loud mob
It bulges, merges, feels with a start alone;
In a bright beam
It waltzes dust to dust with its chance loves.

Of which three souls the praying one is selfless
But only for a span

And the gregarious man's is rudderless, powerless,
While the soul in love is luckless,
Betrays what chance it can.

And still the wind
Blows, the ape is marooned, the lamp ungrasped;
Woman and cat
Still wait to pounce and the climber waits to fall;
As each soul burns
The best it may, in foul or blustering air.
Oh would He, were there a God, have mercy on us all?

PLACE OF A SKULL

Earth water stars and flesh—the seamless coat
Which is the world, he left; who from to-day
Had no more need to wear it. The remote
Metropolis yawned, the parchment flapped away,

Away, and the blood dried in the sand. The bored
Soldiers played for the leavings but even they,
Though trained to carve up continents with the sword,
Approved the weaver who had made night and day

And time and mind a tegument, therefore swore
To hazard it as one lot. The dice were gay
And someone won: *Why the first time I wore
That dead man's coat it frayed I cannot say.*

SLOW MOVEMENT

Waking, he found himself in a train, andante,
With wafers of early sunlight blessing the unknown fields
And yesterday cancelled out, except for yesterday's papers
    Huddling under the seat.

It is still very early, this is a slow movement;
The viola-player's hand like a fish in a glass tank
Rises, remains quivering, darts away
    To nibble invisible weeds.

Great white nebulae lurch against the window
To deploy across the valley, the children are not yet up
To wave us on—we pass without spectators,
    Braiding a voiceless creed.

And the girl opposite, name unknown, is still
Asleep and the colour of her eyes unknown
Which might be wells of sun or moons of wish
    But it is still very early.

The movement ends, the train has come to a stop
In buttercup fields, the fiddles are silent, the whole
Shoal of silver tessellates the aquarium
    Floor, not a bubble rises . . .

And what happens next on the programme we do not know,
If, the red line topped on the gauge, the fish will go mad in
    the tank
Accelerando con forza, the sleeper open her eyes
    And, so doing, open ours.

CAROL

To end all carols, darling,
    To end all carols now,
Let us walk through the cloister
    With a thoughtful brow,

Pruning what was grafted
    Through ages of blind faith—
The rubrics and the finials
    Drift away like breath.

From Bethlehem the sheep-bells
    Grew to a steepled peal,
The joists of the stable
    Spread an ashlar chill,

The rafters of the stable
    Hooped themselves on high
And coveys of boys' voices
    Burst on a stone sky;

While the wrinkled, whimpering image
    Wrapped in his mother's shawl
Was carried between pillars
    Down endless aisles and all

The doors opened before him
    In every holy place
And the doors came to behind him,
    Left him in cold space.

Beyond our prayers and knowing,
    Many light-years away—
So why sing carols, darling?
    To-day is to-day.

Then answered the angel:
  To-day is to-day
And the Son of God is vanished
  But the sons of men stay

And man is a spirit
  And symbols are his meat,
So pull not down the steeple
  In your monied street.

For money chimes feebly,
  Matter dare not sing—
Man is a spirit,
  Let the bells ring.

Ring all your changes, darling,
  Save us from the slough;
Begin all carols, darling,
  Begin all carols now.

THE STYGIAN BANKS

Like a strange soul upon the Stygian banks
Staying for waftage.

TROILUS AND CRESSIDA

(i)

To keep themselves young—Is that why people have children?
To try and catch up with the ghosts of their own discoveries,
A light that has gone into space? Unscrolling history,
To slip back through the New Learning of adolescence
Into those Middle Ages of nursery masons
Where all the bricks were gay; the rondel of the years
Never changing its burden, only the leader
Changing his lines and time changing the leader.
Now it is Spring, O follow your leader, follow your
Child in his fourteenth-century dance; the wool trade
Is booming still, wool is building churches
And the Black Death has not come. Now it is Spring
And the half-grown wheat in the wind is a ripple of satin,
Let you in your child who is only lately articulate
Throw the lassoo of his sight to the height of some green thing,
    christen it
With a new name which no one has ever used
And call a tree a tree.
            Oh, we know that the word merry
Is vulgarized and Chaucer's England was not
All cakes and ale nor all our childhood happy;
Still there is something lost. The very limitedness
Of childhood, its ignorance, its impotence,
Made every cockcrow a miracle after the ogre's night
And every sunbeam glad—as the medieval winter
Slow and dense with cold made March a golden avatar,
April Adam's innocence and May maiden's gaiety;
Nor did the burden change though the blossoms fell,
Alison is for ever aged fifteen
Though leasing different bodies. So let your child

[45]

Bowl your own life in his hoop; a wandering clerk yourself
Have you not in your time stolen a love-song
And written it down in an abbey? A different body
Yours from your father's and your child's from yours
But now it is Spring and the roll of the drums of the Judgement
Muffled with foliage, so you can fool yourself justly,
Playing the jongleur; that your songs are an artifice
Is of your nature; that the blossom must fall
Is what keeps it fresh; that lives and pieces of lives
Are cut off is needed to shape them, time is a chisel,
So what was is. If it were not cut off,
Youth would not be youth. This granted, take your stance
Under the high window which will not open—
You have a right to fool yourself; though your children
Cannot keep either you or themselves young
They *are* themselves in passing and the aubade
Though—no, because—the window will not open
Will find itself in the air, cut off as it must be
By the sudden cry of alarm from the turreted watchman
Which also rhymes. Cut off like a piece of sculpture.
This is the dawn. Reality. Fantasy holds.

(ii)

Fantasy holds the child in the man, the lover in the monk, the
    monk in the lover,
The arbour in the abbey, the ages together,
But as notes are together in music—no merging of history;
The aisles of this church have their intervals. Father and son
Do not repeat; this child has different totems
From that one and from his father's. The slab in the floor of
    the nave
Makes one family a sonnet, each name with a line to itself,
But the lines, however the bones may be jumbled beneath,
Merge no more than the lives did. We must avoid
That haunting wish to fuse all persons together;
To *be* my neighbour is banned—and if I could be,

[46]

I could neither know him nor love him. Each of us carries
His own ground with him to walk on. Look at your child
Bowling his hoop along that arterial road
Where he cannot read the signpost; as he trundles,
It may, as they say, ring some bell from your past
Or, as Aristotle would put it, by an analogy
Match his private theme with themes of your own
As a waft of roses for one, of beans for another,
Will waft him back not to a general love
But to some girl with a name, herself and no other.
Analogy, correspondence, metaphor, harmonics—
We have no word for the bridges between our present
Selves and our past selves or between ourselves and others
Or between one part of ourselves and another part,
Yet we must take it as spoken, the bridge is there
Or how could your child's hoop cross it? Strike the right note
And the wine-glasses will ring. I am alone
And you are alone and he and she are alone
But in that we carry our grounds we can superimpose them,
No more fusing them than a pack of cards is fused
Yet the Jack comes next to the Queen. Though when they are
      dealt
You will often fail of the sequence; only you know
That there were such cards in the pack, there *are* other people
And moss-roses and beanfields and in yourself
Monk and lover and a battered hoop
With you for once behind it—and a coffin
With you for once within it. All these active,
Even that idol of wax which now it is Spring
Jogs your elbow as the blossom falls
Whispering: 'Fulfil yourself. But renounce the temptation
To imbrue the world with self and thus blaspheme
All other selves by merging them. Rather fill,
Fulfil yourself with the Give and Take of the Spring
And honour the green of the grass, the rights of the others,
Taking what they can give, giving what they can take,
Not random pigments muddled and puddled together

[47]

But a marriage of light reflected.' Thus the figure
Who has retired, warning against retiring
Now it is Spring and the roll of the drums of the Judgement
Can still be assumed far off. The hoops are running
A cow-parsley gauntlet, white as though for a wedding,
Alison is fifteen, the labourer's arm
Ripples with muscle, the green corn with wind,
And the glasses chime to a note that we cannot hear
For the frequency is too high. Within us a monk
Copies a love-song but remains a monk
And out there beyond our eyes Tom-Dick-and-Harry
Remain respectively Tom and Dick and Harry
Clapping backs in the sunshine. Granted the word merry
Is out of favour, it is the word's fault;
The thing itself yet sprouts and spouts before you
Calling for a communion. Fill your glasses;
When they are emptied again, the note may be higher yet
And your own glass may break.

(iii)

And what when the glass breaks when the Note sounds?
What when the wind blows and the bough breaks?
Will each life seem a lullaby cut off
And no humanity adult? From the tree-top
Where all our conversation was *Why* and *Mine*
The answer now being *Why Not? Not Yours!*
If so, if we have by a sense no right to be here,
Trespassers, propertyless, never of age,
Branded by thoughts, born with a silver spoon—
With the power of words—in the mouth and smuggling in
To a world of foregone conclusions the heresy of choice,
If, to sum all, to be born man is wrong,
Breaking a closed circle, then let us break it clean
And make two wrongs a right, using the contraband
The genes got past the customs, putting it out at interest
And in the face of Nature's ritual of reflex actions

[48]

Riding our heresy high. Look, love! Now it is Spring
And the wind blows, pick what buds you fancy,
Fill your wine-glass, rockabye baby, break the circular world
    wide open;
It is your birthright never to be grown up
But always growing, never yourself completed
As are the brutes and therefore, unlike the brutes,
Able to shape something outside yourself
Finding completion only in othernesses
Whether perceived started without you
Or conceived within you, ending beyond you;
For things that you do or make can win a final pattern
But never yourself—never at least until
The velocity of a wind, the frequency of a note,
End in a topple, a clink, a shutter released
And the dead man gets his exposure. But now it is Spring
And we need not be camera-conscious, we are still doing and
    making
Not to display our muscles but to elicit
A rhythm, a value, implicit in something beyond us.
Rockabye baby! The wind that whitens the cornfield
And lilts in the telephone wires is tilting the tree-top
Further and further—but sing in your cradle,
You can outplay that wind which cutting off your song
Can never cut off itself, merely repeats itself
Where yours will end and find itself in the air
Unlike your body not returning to earth
But There—like a piece of sculpture.
                            Yes, let the teacher of ethics
Reduce all acts to selfishness, let the economist
Confuse conditions and causes and the psychologist
Prove and disprove the rose from manure and the scientist
Explain all value away by material fact—
What do I care? It is Spring and it always will be
However the blossoms fall; and however impure
Our human motives, we can sheer off sometimes
On the purity of a tangent. Let the wind

[49]

Lunge like a trombone, draw back his hand to his mouth,
Then lunge again and further; he is welcome
And time and all particulars are welcome
And death which rounds the song. Fill your glasses;
There *is* a distinction between vintages
· And heretics must have courage. There *is* a despair
Which the animals do not know, it is chiefly exhaustion
When the bull kneels down in the ring; but our despair
Need not exhaust, it is our privilege—
Our paradox—to recognize the insoluble
And going up with an outstretched hand salute it.
For we, unlike the bull, have a matador within us
More titivated still, more cruel still,
Whom we have known for years and the holiday crowd
Have been waiting there for years and the sand is smooth
And the sun will not go in till the show is over. Yes,
We too are in a ring and gaudy banderillas
May quiver in our flanks; the paradox
Is that we can break out—being about to die
We can salute our death, the consciousness
Of what must be ennobling that arena
Where we have defied what must be.
                                        Now it is Spring
And the blossoms fall like sighs but we can hold them
Each as a note in the air, a chain of defiance,
Making the transient last by having Seen it
And so distilled value from mere existence;
· Thus when our own existence is cut off
That stroke will put a seal upon our value.
The eye will close but the vision that it borrowed
Has sealed the roses red.

(iv)

That roses are red is home—and homesickness.
As that men are alive is living—and deathwish;
And that men are dead is a name and a cause.
The hoop takes different turnings, Alison different bodies,

The burden does not change;
Though the spokesman may simulate progress
It must be within that unchanging framework,
Drilling the peas and beans in the garden but not seeing over
    the wall,
The mellow grass-grown wall encircling and forbidding
Too high to climb and no birds fly across it;
Only an incoming wind which unlike the winds of the garden
(The winds which threaten the new-born child in the tree-top
But only can share the name of This by analogy)
Flutters no paper tag on a stick in a plot,
Moves no leaf; the dandelion puffballs
Ignore it and we often. Often—but why are that lover's
Eyes of a sudden distant? He does not raise them—
One cannot see over the wall—Not one hair on his head
Is blown out of place but he ceases to give, give out;
Does not even widen his focus for here is
A movement only inwards, intake of distance.
Until she speaks and the wall is back in its place
Rounding off their vision again with words,
Unchanging burden to which the bees assent
And the thrush with a snail in its beak. A 'real' wind
Yawns—and flicks a tree-top nonchalantly
As if to say 'Look, though half in my sleep,
I can do more than that Other.' So all is well. As it was.
The voices of pigeons are grinding their delicate mills of lust,
Arkwright and Hargreaves are busy changing England,
The hooter sounds at eight, Darwin will sweep away
One code and give us a new one; all is well
As the girl sees in her lover's eyes returning—
'I am so glad you are here. I am so glad you are back.
Now you must stay for ever. Do not be foolish;
Even if a wind from over the wall can reach you,
It is a one-way traffic.' And saying this she smiles
And smiling this she lies and lying knows it,
There is a fleck of distance in her eyes too,
But the mill must grind. Why is it people have children?

So take London to-day: the queues of itching minds
Waiting for news that they do not want, for nostrums
They only pretend to believe in; most of their living
Is grinding mills that are not even their own.
The pigeons are luckier in their significant ritual,
And the dome of Saint Paul's more overt in its significance
But what to these does the word significant signify,
Who are neither autonomous crystals nor willing notes
In any symphonic whole? What they achieve of value
Is mainly in spasms, might be ascribed to chance
Did we not know that all men, even apparent ciphers,
Rough out their own best moments. Moments too rare
For most of these in the queue. Granted the garden,
There are distinctions in soil and in what comes out of it
(To consider means is not mean, so long as a gadget
Is not set up for an end, so long as an end
Can infiltrate into means); but still, above all,
To raise a value gardens must be gardened
Which is where choice comes in. Then will. Then sweat.
And—in the last resort—there is something else comes in
That does not belong and yet—You see that wall?
Many will tell you that is what protects us,
What makes in fact the garden, saves it from not-being
So that, now it is there, we need not think beyond it;
But look at the eyes of that tired man in the queue
In whom fatigue dulling the senses has rendered
Some other part of him sensitive—Intake of distance.
What is it that comes in? Can it be that the wall
Is really a stepping-stone? So that what is beyond it
(That which as well perhaps could be called what is Not)
Is the sanction itself of the wall and so of the garden?
Do we owe these colours and shapes to something which seems
        their death?
It does not bear thinking of; that was not a thought came in
To the tired man's eyes—Look back at him now; he has lost it,
Perhaps we only imagined that *he* imagined—
No matter, the queue is moving. Move along there;

If you want a system the public address is a good one
And you need not ask how came this mechanical voice
Nor by what right it tells you to move along there.
The blue cock pigeon is courting again. The hooter
Will sound at eight. That is the end of the news.

(v)

That is the end of the news. The humanist
Thinks he has heard something new and the man in the street
Passing the garish but dowdy hoarding dodges the dripping brush
While his brother changes the posters. Now it is Spring
But the know-all blonde on the poster will never know it
For only a few projections of human minds
Are able to give and take. For all that, now it is Spring—
Foaming white edges of roads, white hedges, white
Alison walking the rim of a classical text
Lovingly copied by monks who misunderstood it
But in her arms are flowers, long hours of flowers,
And her smile serene as young and the horned head-dress
Cuts the enamel sky. People have children,
One might say, to be childish. Munching salad
Your child can taste the colour itself—the green—
And the colour of radish—the red; his jaded parents,
Wise to the fallacy, foster it (for we begin with
A felt unity and, they presume, shall end with
An unfelt ditto but all between is by proxy,
So the more mouthfuls of cress he takes the better,
For *we* can remember . . . can we? . . .) Glory is what?
The remembrance of an effulgence that was illusion?
Or is the illusion now in burnishing the past?
Or building up, in the catch-phrase, for the future
Which, with a capital F, is a catch-phrase too? Nostalgia
Implies having a home. Which heroes die for—
But can they without having seen it? The hackneyed songs
Mislead us—Home Sweet Rose, Last Home of Summer—
The paradox of a sentimentalist

Insisting on clinging to what he insists is gone;
When now is the opposite paradox now it is Spring
And what we insist remains we insist on leaving
After exchange of courtesies. Let the blossom
Fall, that is fact but the fact can be retranslated
To value of blossom and also to value of fall;
While we, who recognize both, must turn our backs on the
    orchard
To follow the road of facts which we make ourselves
Where others, men, will help us to conjure value
In passing and out of passing but always turning
Our backs on the road we have made
Until—which has value too—at a certain point we fall
And the hoop topples into the ditch. The well-worn symbols
Of quests and inns and pilgrims' progresses
Do correspond; the inn-sign clanks in the night
And the windows gild the cobbles—which is merry,
All the more because we meet it in transit
And the next morning Tom and Dick as to-day
May clap each other on the back and Harry may still stare down
Into the tawny well in the pewter mug—
Or so we think having left them but in fact
They too are for the road, they too have heard
The roll of recruiting drums beyond the horizon
However the woods of spring may blur the reverberations
As in the little church the fresco above the rood-loft
Has lost its percussive colours but though faded
The bearded Judge and the horned figures with prongs
Unlike the blonde in the poster still can give. And take.

(vi)

And take me then! In the dawn under the high window
The burden is the same. And on the black embankment
The lost man watching the lights jig in the water
And choosing the spot to plunge has the same burden
But the lines between are gone; his own invention

[54]

They slipped his memory sooner. So the lover,
Once the watchman cries, must kiss his hand
Up to the grille and go. And the lisping child
Envious of a bird stretches his arms to fly
Or to embrace the sea, loving it at first sight:
O air, O water, take me! Thus there are some
Who when the wind which is not like any wind known
Brings to their ears from ahead the drums of the Judgement
Slacken their pace and, not to be taken by That,
Implore all others to take them. As if those others could answer
In the absolute terms required. It is only silence
Could answer them as they want, only the wind
Which they dread, the wind which passes Alison by
Without even ruffling her dress, yet once in a way
Passes not by but into her. Ancient Athens
Was a sparrow-chatter of agora-gibes and eristic
But in the mind of Socrates beneath
His quizzical voice was the daemon, a cone of silence;
And in Imperial Rome in the roaring bloody arena
Linking the man with the net and the man with the sword
Was a circuit of silence, electric. The Middle Ages
Were rowdy with earth and hell, yet in Alison's poise in the
    orchard,
Dripping from the pen of the monk, the lance of the Lanz-
    knecht,
Was a silence, drop by drop. But here to-day in London
Can we—we cannot have—lost it? Talking so much
Our optimism and pessimism are both
Corrupted dialects, divorced from grammar,
Almost indeed from meaning. The hooter sounds,
The busker sings to the queue, grinding of gears,
But if we stopped haggling, stopped as we did in the raids,
The gap in our personal racket, as in the gunfire,
Should become positive, crystal; which is the end of the news
Which is the beginning of wisdom. No captions and no jargon,
No diminution, distortion or sterilization of entity,
But calling a tree a tree. For this wisdom

Is not an abstraction, a wordiness, but being silence
Is love of the chanting world.

(vii)

So let the world chant on. There is harsh fruit in the garden
But flowers are flowers and, what is more, can be tended
And here we stay and communicate, joining hands
To share the burden while each in turn can throw
His own lines in between; friar and wandering tumbler
Smuggle a pollen of culture into the villages
And Socrates stands by the sun-dial, talking away
But his soul is calm, moving, not seeming to move,
Like the pointer of shadow and silent. Yes, here we stay—for
    a little—
Strange souls in the daylight. Troilus
Patrols the Stygian banks, eager to cross,
But the value is not on the further side of the river,
The value lies in his eagerness. No communion
In sex or elsewhere can be reached and kept
Perfectly or for ever. The closed window,
The river of Styx, the wall of limitation
Beyond which the word beyond loses its meaning,
Are the fertilizing paradox, the grille
That, severing, joins, the end to make us begin
Again and again, the infinite dark that sanctions
Our growing flowers in the light, our having children;
The silence behind our music. The very silence
Which the true martyr hears on the pyre to darken
The hissing motley flames and the jeers, to make him
In spite of logic a phoenix. From that silence
Are borrowed ear and voice and from that darkness
We borrow vision, seal the roses red.
The hooter will sound at eight till the wall falls
But in the meantime—which is time—it is ours
To practise a faith which is heresy and by defying
Our nature to raise a flag on it. Come, let us laugh

As the animals cannot, laugh in the mind for joy;
Let the west wind lather the tree-top, toss the cradle,
Let the young decant the spring for us, banners of wine
While the Jack sits next to the Queen, let us busily gaily
Build us a paean, mixing for need is the metaphors,
Munching the green and the red, becoming as little children
Whose curls are falling blossom, using the eye
And the ear to fill the orchestra, plant the garden,
Bowling a hoop, braiding a love-song, fighting
A fire that cannot be seen; heretics all
Who unlike anything else that breathes in the world
When feeling pain can be lyrical and despairing
Can choose what we despair of. Glory is what?
We cannot answer in words though every verb is a hint of it
And even Die is a live word. Nor can we answer
In any particular action for each is adulterate coin
However much we may buy with it. No answer
Is ours—yet we are unique
In putting the question at all and a false coin
Presumes a true mint somewhere. Your child's hoop,
Though far from a perfect circle, holds the road
And the road is far from straight, yet like a bee
Can pollinate the towns for the towns though ugly
Have blossom in them somewhere. Far from perfect
Presumes perfection *where?* A catechism the drums
Asseverate day-long, night-long: Glory is what?
A question! . . . Now it is Spring.

LETTER FROM INDIA
for Hedli

Our letters cross by nosing silver
Place of a skull, skull of a star,
Each answer coming late and little,
The air-mail being no avatar,
And whence I think I know you are
I feel divided as for ever.

For here where men as fungi burgeon
And each crushed puffball dies in dust
This plethoric yet phantom setting
Makes yours remote so that even lust
Can take no tint nor curve on trust
Beyond these plains' beyondless margin.

You are north-west but what is Western
Assurance here where words are snakes
Gulping their tails, flies that endemic
In mosque and temple, morgue and jakes,
Eat their blind fill of man's mistakes
And yet each carcase proves eternal?

Here where the banyan weeps her children,
Where pavements flower with wounds and fins
And kite and vulture hold their vigil
Which never ends, never begins
To end, this world which spins and grins
Seems a mere sabbath of bacilli;

So that, for all the beauties hoarded
In Buddhist stupa, Mogul tomb,
In flick of hand and fold of sari,
In chant and scripture which illume
The soul's long night, I find no room
For our short night in this miasma

Where smiling, sidling, cuddling hookahs
They breed and broil, breed and brawl,
Their name being legend while their lifewish
Verging on deathwish founders all
This colour in one pool, one pall,
Granting no incense and no lotus.

Whereas though Europe founder likewise
Too close acquaintance leaves us blind
Who by aloofness, by selection,
Have written off what looms behind
The fragile fences of our mind,
Have written off the flood, the jungle.

So cast up here this India jolts us
Awake to what engrossed our sleep;
This was the truth and now we see it,
This was the horror—it is deep;
The lid is off, the things that creep
Down there are we, we were there always.

And always also, doubtless, ruthless
Doubt made us grope for the same clue,
We too sat cross-legged, eyes on navel,
Deaf to the senses and we too
Saw the Beyond—but now the view
Is of the near, the too near only.

I have seen Sheikhupura High School
Fester with glaze-eyed refugees
And the bad coin of fear inverted
Under Purana Kila's trees
And like doomed oxen those and these
Cooped by their past in a blind circle;

And day by day, night upon nightmare,
Have spied old faults and sores laid bare,

Line upon lineless, measureless under
Pretended measure, and no air
To feed such premises as where
A private plot would warrant shelter.

For even should humanism always
Have been half-impotent, debased,
How for all that can her own children
Break from the retina encased
In which our vision here must waste,
Meeting but waste, the chance of Vision?

And a Testator half-forgotten
Still with his will sways you and me
Presuming Jack and Jill so sacred
That though all rivers reach the sea
His course through land's diversity
Is still for us what makes a river.

What wonder then if from this maelstrom
Of persons where no person counts
I should feel frail trusting the ether
With love in weighed and staid amounts
And as the liaising aircraft mounts
Can think its chartered speed illusion?

For though to me an absolute person
Yet even you and even by me
Being clamped by distance in a burga
Cannot be seen, still less can see
How in this earlier century
Dark children daub the skies with arson.

And the small noises that invest me,
The sweepers' early morning slow
Swishing, the electric fans, the crickets,
Plait a dense hedge between us so

That your voice rings of long ago,
Beauty asleep in a Grimm story.

Yet standing here and notwithstanding
Our severance, need I think it loss
If from this past you are my future
As in all spite of gulf and gloss
However much their letters cross
East and West are wed and welcome;

And both of us are both, in either
An India sleeps below our West,
So you for me are proud and finite
As Europe is, yet on your breast
I could find too that undistressed
East which is east and west and neither?

October 1947